This Book Belongs To:

THE FIRST CHRISTMAS CAROL

TL SCHAEFER

ILLUSTRATION BY KENNEDY WALDROP

To my kids, Ruth and Simon.

My loves, dare to hope with abandon and live like
Christmas is always tomorrow morning.
God hopes like that too.

'Twas the night of first Christmas,
and all through the stable.

Not an animal was stirring.
Nor person nor angel.

Outside was warm.
Not a snowflake did fall.

No snow in Bethlehem. No.
None at all.

STARS STRUNG TOGETHER LIKE JOLLY BRIGHT LIGHTS
GLOWING AND GUIDING TO THIS HOLIEST OF NIGHTS

MAGI CAME HOPEFUL, WITH GIFTS UNDER EACH ARM
BRAVING A JOURNEY FULL OF UNKNOWN AND HARM

SO WAS THE NIGHT OF A PROPHECY
BEING FULFILLED. WISEMEN. GIFTS. AND
SHEPHERDS OF THE FIELD.

WHO CRAWLED O'ER MOUNTAIN TOPS,
TO THE STRANGEST OF LAND. TO A
VIRGIN BIRTH. AND TO A PERFECT
LITTLE MAN.

No stockings that night. No ornaments. Nor toys.
Just a mom a dad. And sweet baby boy.
There. In that stable. He slept where sheep fed.
And right there he lay. Upon a cozy hay bed

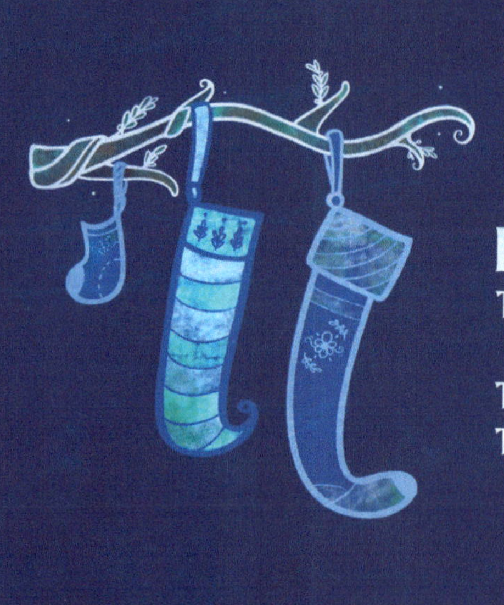

His eyes softly open. Cheeks rosy and red.
The true King of Kings born in the animals' shed.

Through that first night, he'd fuss and he'd cry.
The Lord of Lords had come to be as you and I.

He lay there like a gift.
With no ribbons nor bows.
Perfection cooing sweet.
And wiggling new toes.

A baby given to us all. A gift
for you and for me.

The first Christmas present.
Born to be hung on a tree.

His momma kissing his head. Needing no mistletoe.
She'd watch this small boy mature. Learn and then
grow.

Her boy would. One day. Heal the blind. Fix the lame.
He would ease all our pain. And erase all our shame.

'Twas the night of eternal forgiveness and sweet.
sweet. grace. Twas little arms. Little legs. And a soft
baby's face.

Our gift from a father. And chance to be saved. Our
promise of rescue. And our debts all forgiven and paid.

As he lay in that manger,
taking first earthly breath,

This hero of life, would someday
be champion of death.

He was made into something he
did not yet know, the high king,
for our sake, born here quite low.

Joy lives in his birth, and the resolve
of his promise, peace is his spirit, and
how it does call us.

Hope is his body, like bread it
was broken, love is his legacy,
and future to hope in.

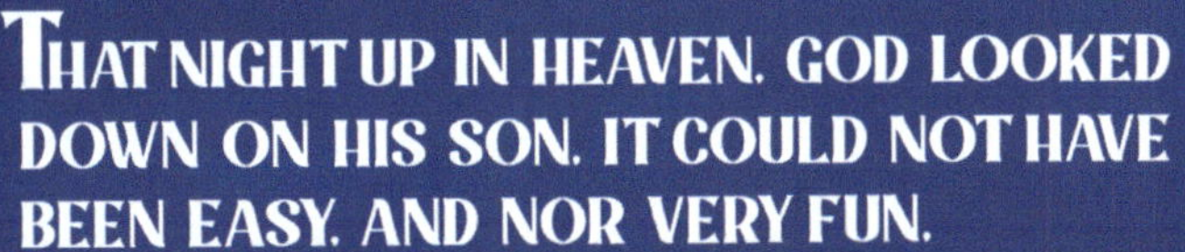

That night up in heaven, God looked
down on his son. It could not have
been easy, and nor very fun.

As a new mother watched Jesus,
asleep in that manger.

Her baby brought into a world of
such chaos and danger.

God said aloud, "Take my son, and hold
tight. See his perfection, acknowledge
his might. This gift I give to you, so we
may be right. To man and to woman,
and each child alike.

Merry Christmas to all,
and to all a good night."

The End